LIVING BIG
IN SMALL APARTMENTS

LIVING BIG
IN SMALL APARTMENTS

JAMES GRAYSON TRULOVE

HD

Harper
DESIGN

An Imprint of HarperCollins*Publishers*

Living Big in Small Apartments

Copyright 2005 © by James Grayson Trulove and HARPER DESIGN

Published in 2005 by:
Harper Design
An Imprint of HarperCollins*Publishers*
10 East 53rd Street
New York, NY 10022
Tel: (212) 207-7000
Fax: (212) 207-7654
HarperDesign@harpercollins.com
www.harpercollins.com

Distributed throughout the world by:
HarperCollins International
10 East 53rd Street
New York, NY 10022
Fax: (212) 207-7654

HarperCollins books may be purchased for educational, business, or sales promotional use.
For information, please write: Special Markets Department, HarperCollins Publishers Inc.,
10 East 53rd Street, New York, NY 10022.

Packaged by:
Grayson Publishing, LLC
James G. Trulove, Publisher
1250 28th Street NW
Washington, DC 20007
202-337-1380
jtrulove@aol.com
Graphic Design by: Agnieszka Stachowicz

Library of Congress Control Number: 2005922571

ISBN: 0-06-077998-5

Manufactured in China
First printing, 2005
1 2 3 4 5 6 7 8 9 / 08 07 06 05

Contents

FOREWORD

SMALL IS A RELATIVE TERM WHEN DESCRIBING A LIVING SPACE. IT IS dependent upon the way in which the space will be used: is it for occasional visits to the city or a full-time residence; is it just for sleeping or will it need to function as a live/work space or a place for entertaining? Geography plays an important part in determining what is small: a small apartment in New York or Tokyo might be regarded as a closet in Dallas. And it is dependent on the number of people who will be living there: a single person, a couple, or a family. In general, studio apartments are under 500 square feet; one bedroom apartments are under 1000 square feet; and small two bedroom apartments and lofts are well south of 2000 square feet. In my previous book on the subject of small apartments, *Big Ideas for Small Spaces: Studio Apartments*, the focus was on the smallest of the small. For this book, I decided to extend the range and look at typical small apartments and lofts that would be found in most densely populated urban environments, from studios to small two bedrooms.

In each case, and regardless of the floor plan, the apartments chosen for this book have one thing in common: space is at a premium and the architects were challenged to make every square foot count. Sometimes the spaces are full of potential, with lots of light and high ceilings. In other cases, living, eating, sleeping, and entertaining must be crammed into a single, narrow space with natural light at a premium. What is most apparent when reviewing the eighteen apartments in this book is that there are scores of ideas for turning the most modest of apartments into laboratories for comfortable living, and for dealing with the most difficult and typical of design problems where size is but one consideration.

ABOVE: In the Lucas Loft, a thick plaster wall runs the length of the apartment, serving as an anchor for furniture, as a privacy wall for the sleeping area, and as a place to display art.

RIGHT: The White Space apartment is all about maximizing the view in a minimalist environment.

LEFT: In the Seidmon Apartment, the challenge was to bring natural light to the windowless rear. The solution was to use translucent walls.

ABOVE: Similarly, in the NoHo Loft, a translucent bookcase wall allows natural light to filter into the bedroom.

LEFT: In the Thompson Street apartment, the bathroom is fully drained, allowing for a larger bathing space.

BELOW: Many small apartments have open kitchens. In the McGrath Apartment, the stainless steel kitchen can be essentially closed when not in use.

9

PROJECTS

FREEMAN APARTMENT

ARCHITECT **Belmont Freeman Architects** PHOTOGRAPHER **Christopher Wesnofske**

THE ARCHITECT'S OWN RESIDENCE IS A COMBINATION of two apartments—a small one-bedroom and a studio—and two terraces with unobstructed views.

The plan for the renovation was to open up the small rooms into a single, flowing space and to capitalize on the abundant light and views. A new kitchen was built at the west end of the apartment, screened from the living room by a partial-height wall. Distance and the curvature of the floor plan separate the bedroom from the public space with no need for a door. Closets and a bathroom open off the passageway from living room to bedroom. New, oversized glass sliding doors open onto the terraces.

To create a feeling of serene unity, the entire apartment is rendered in just four materials: white-painted plaster walls and ceilings, white plastic laminate cabinetry, stainless-steel countertops in the kitchen and bath, and a blue-gray terrazzo floor. Furniture is kept equally spare. A vintage 1949 George Nelson daybed defines the living area. The architect designed the dining table (which doubles as a desk), the leather ottoman, and the built-in cabinetry in the living room that conceals video and sound equipment.

PREVIOUS PAGES: A
spare palette of materials
and furnishings and a
great view create a
dramatic urban space.

RIGHT: A carefully placed
mirror in the bathroom
reflects the view from
the terrace.

Floor Plan

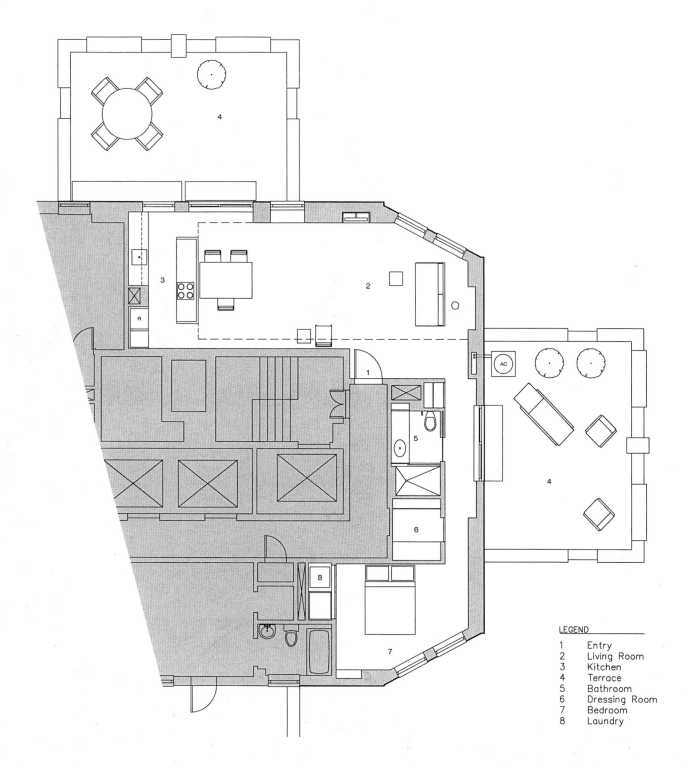

LEGEND

1	Entry
2	Living Room
3	Kitchen
4	Terrace
5	Bathroom
6	Dressing Room
7	Bedroom
8	Laundry

LEFT: The entry and
corridor to the bedroom as
seen from the living area

LEFT: A partial wall separates the living and dining area from the kitchen.

FAR LEFT: Stainless steel countertops adorn the minimalist kitchen.
LEFT: The corridor connecting the living area with the bedroom
FOLLOWING PAGES: One of two terraces dramatically extends the apartment to the outside.

5TH AVENUE LOFT

ARCHITECT Chelsea Atelier PHOTOGRAPHER Björg Magnea

THIS PROJECT CONSISTED OF REDESIGNING A TYPICAL New York apartment into a live and work loft. The design goal was to soften the barriers within the space by replacing solid walls with translucent glass walls and linking the apartment together via visual clues. The bedroom is designed as an extension of the living room, but can be separated from it by large sliding glass doors. The kitchen is left open and is separated from the bathroom by a colored transparent glass wall.

In the kitchen, white Carrara marble is used extensively, outlining the island counter and stretching across the wall to form a continuous backsplash. Wine bottles are stacked within an amber-colored cast resin wine rack that extends vertically above the counter top. The bathroom walls are covered in French limestone with shallow sandstone sinks that project out of the stone wall, concealing the laundry room. A large shower area defined by clear glass walls is designed for two and fitted with separate spray heads.

PREVIOUS PAGES: The
dark Brazilian cherry
floors provide a welcome
contrast to the cool
marble and stainless
steel kitchen.

Floor Plan

ENRTY

HALLWAY

STORAGE

KITCHEN

REF

DW

W/D

BATHROOM

LIVING ROOM

SLIDING DOORS

BEDROOM

CL

LEFT: An oversized storage closet is an added bonus for a small apartment.
ABOVE: The amber-colored cast resin wine rack

FOLLOWING PAGES: A view of the living area and bedroom from the kitchen

LEFT AND ABOVE: Cool minimalism defines the marble and stainless steel kitchen, which also benefits from a window over the sink.

LEFT AND RIGHT: The bedroom is designed as an extension of the living area. The large translucent glass doors can separate the two spaces without sacrificing the sense of light and space typical of a loft.

ABOVE: The limestone sinks in the bathroom project from the wall that conceals the laundry room.
RIGHT: The walls of the bathroom are French limestone.

APARTMENT II

ARCHITECT Stephen Alton PHOTOGRAPHER Eduard Hueber/Archphoto

THIS APARTMENT IS LOCATED ONE FLOOR BELOW Apartment 22 (page 44). And while both apartments are identical in size and configuration, it is interesting to see how the same architect was able to create two totally different designs and moods.

The restrained color palette and the finishes of the apartment give it an industrial feel. A freestanding storage and media unit separates the bedroom from the living area. It is made of limed quarter-sawn oak with a glassed space above and sliding glass doors to provide privacy for the bedroom. A custom bookshelf covered in linen is also located in the living area and a built-in office is tucked behind doors off the dining area. The bathroom has a waxed concrete finish and the kitchen counters are soapstone with stainless-steel appliances. The floor is raised concrete.

Floor Plan

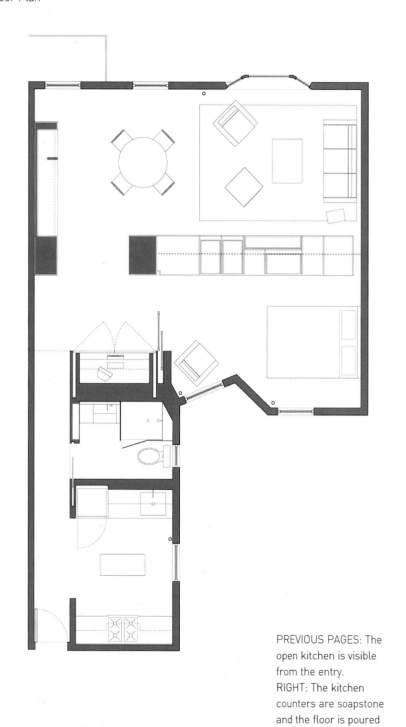

PREVIOUS PAGES: The open kitchen is visible from the entry.
RIGHT: The kitchen counters are soapstone and the floor is poured concrete.

RIGHT: A free-standing
storage wall of quarter-
sawn oak separates the
living and dining areas
from the bedroom.
FOLLOWING PAGES:
Opposite the storage wall,
the bedroom is accessed
via sliding translucent
doors; the ultramodern
bathroom has a waxed
concrete finish.

APARTMENT 22

ARCHITECT **Stephen Alton** PHOTOGRAPHER **Eduard Hueber/Archphoto**

THIS APARTMENT IS LOCATED ONE FLOOR ABOVE Apartment 11 (page 36). New construction included reconfiguration of doors to the bedroom, bathroom, and kitchen. Hidden storage is located at end of the living room where the surface of the closet doors were developed as floating white planes, each having a different directional and surface angle. Pink translucent sliding doors are used to separate the living room from the bedroom and bathroom. A special film allows for clarity when viewed from an angle but is otherwise opaque. This voyeuristic element was also explored in the treatment of the shower stall and the pivoting faceted mirrors in the bathroom. A custom-poured epoxy sink lit from below extends from the mirrored wall in the bathroom.

The lighting in all areas of the apartment is positioned to illuminate the surfaces of walls that either have moving objects below, such as cabinet doors, or have faceted surfaces so that the shadows emphasize their three-dimensional quality. Cove lighting along the entrance hall provides illumination for art work and makes the hall appear wider.

PREVIOUS PAGES AND
RIGHT: Random panels on
the hidden storage closets
in the living room function
as a work of art.

BELOW: Detail of lighting
above the faceted mirror
in the bathroom

Floor Plan

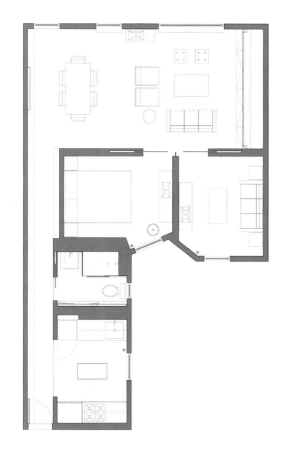

ABOVE AND RIGHT: A translucent scrim covers the window in the all white kitchen.

LEFT: Cove lighting in the entry hall makes the space appear wider. ABOVE: A faceted mirror runs the length of the bathroom.

RIGHT: The custom-poured epoxy sink in the bathroom is lit from the floor.

LUCAS LOFT

ARCHITECT Stephen Chung, Kamran Zahedi PHOTOGRAPHER Stephen M. Lee

THIS LOFT RENOVATION FOR AN ART COLLECTOR IS located within a metal "bridge" that spans two former industrial buildings. Because of this, the loft's two party walls are the original exterior walls of the two brick buildings. As a result, the walls have a weathered character and offer a dramatic contrast with the finely crafted interior. A glass wall at the north end of the bridge brings light deep into the open space.

In order to retain the loft-like quality of the space, the architect developed a scheme that relies on minimal intervention, with no walls reaching the ceiling except to enclose the bathroom. A low, thick plaster wall running north-south is carefully modulated to create niches for the display of art objects and areas for built-in furniture. A maple veneer "wrapper" folds around the perimeter of the space, beginning as kitchen cabinets and continuing as a flat plane along the brick walls with added niches for display space for the owner's art collection. Most of the furniture and fixtures in the loft were designed by local craftsmen specifically for the space.

Floor Plan

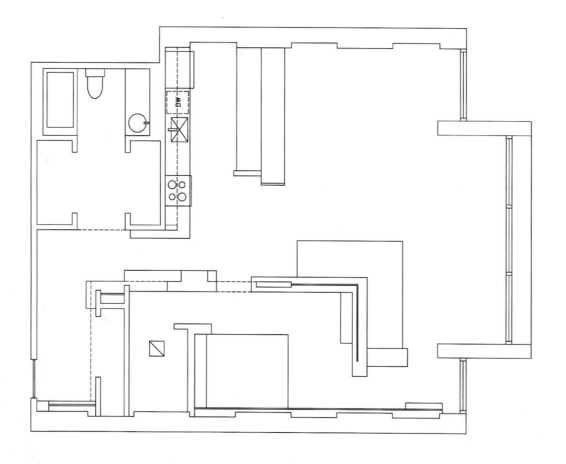

PREVIOUS PAGES AND LEFT: The maple veneer wall begins as cabinets in the kitchen and continues its journey around the perimeter of the apartment, adding warmth to the space.

LEFT AND ABOVE: The plaster wall encloses the bedroom while providing an anchor for built-in furniture and works of art.

FOLLOWING PAGES: A view into the bedroom from the kitchen; the kitchen as seen from the bedroom.

THOMPSON STREET STUDIO

ARCHITECT Tang Kawasaki Studio **PHOTOGRAPHER** Björg Magnea

IN MANHATTAN, WHERE APARTMENT DESIGN IS OFTEN a never ending challenge to put a maximum amount of utility into a minimum amount of space, the architects for the renovation of this studio took the challenge to a new level. The owner, a film director, needed this under 400-square-foot space to function as both a home and workspace. So in addition to the usual domestic activities of cooking, eating, sleeping, bathing, and entertaining, he also needed a screening room, a digital workspace, and storage for the accompanying audio-visual equipment.

The design solution is a clever now-you-see-it, now-you-don't approach in which the apartment is transformed, depending on its current usage. When the Murphy bed is in place, translucent glass doors seal it off from the kitchen area. With the bed up, a motorized projection screen converts the same space into a screening room. Storage is maximized by taking advantage of this typical tenement building's haphazard geometry. An independent system of floor-to-ceiling, offset-pivot doors conceals pullout closets and trolleys that also become furniture, when needed.

A subdued palette of materials that include white concrete, glass, white lacquered doors and millwork, and dark bronze epoxy painted wood floors enhances the play of light and space, aided by careful attention to the placement of artificial lighting throughout the apartment.

PREVIOUS PAGES: A white wall of full-height lacquered doors contains an extraordinary amount of storage space.

LEFT: The bathroom is fully drained in order to maximize the use of the space. A translucent glass door brings light into the small space while adding a sense of depth to the apartment. The shower enclosure, the vanity basin, and the kitchen counter with its integrated sink are all made of custom white concrete.

BELOW: An independent system of floor-to-ceiling offset pivot doors conceals pullout closets and trolleys that act as furniture. Here, the closets can be seen in the closed and open positions.

South Elevation with closet doors closed

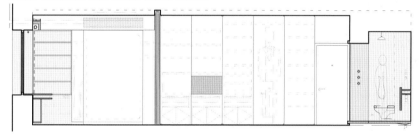

South Elevation with closet doors open

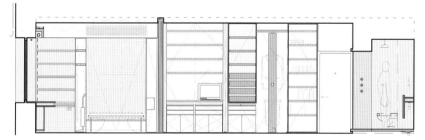

North Elevation

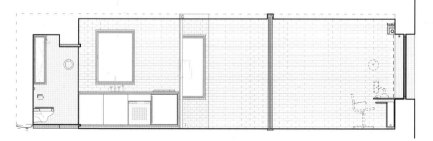

Floor Plan

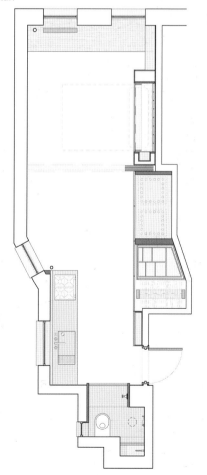

LEFT: When the Murphy bed is down, the public space becomes private. Translucent, sliding glass doors make the space more intimate while allowing light from the two end windows to enter the rest of the apartment. RIGHT: A motorized projection screen converts the same space into a screening room and it also serves as a blackout shade against eastern exposures.

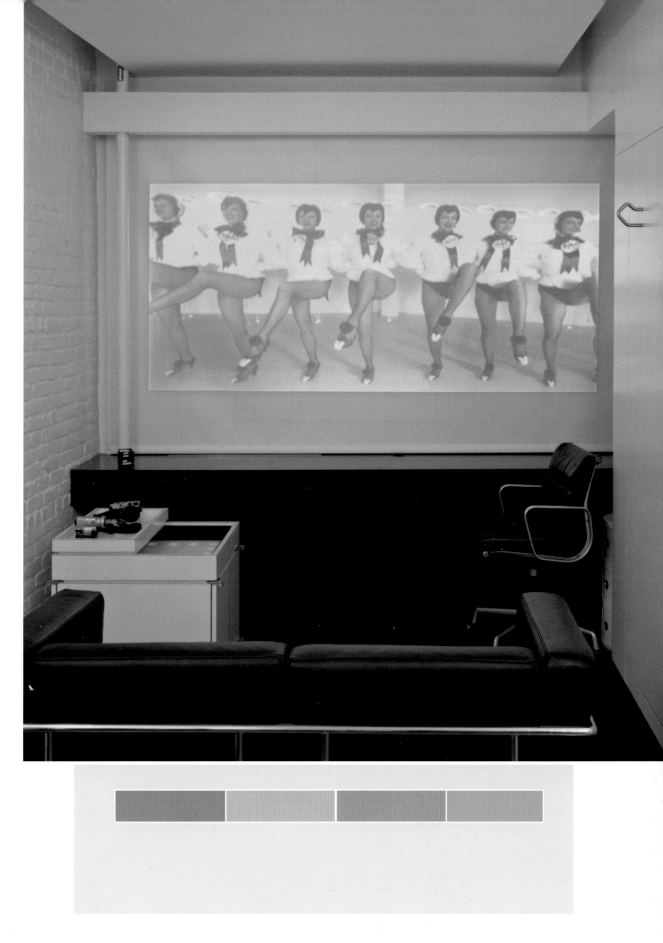

LEFT: When the bed and screen are up, the space is transformed into a living room.

LEHR APARTMENT

ARCHITECT Anima **PHOTOGRAPHY** Paúl Rivera/Archphoto

THE COMBINATION OF TWO SIDE-BY-SIDE STUDIO apartments in this former West Village hotel provided the unique envelope for this residence. Owned by a collector of American Arts & Crafts furniture, the space was designed as both a new family residence and showroom for selected antiques.

Fortunately, the apartments have high ceilings, so in order to gain more floor space, a new mezzanine platform was constructed over about half of the apartment. The other half was left open to the high ceilings and contains a living room and dining room. A stainless steel kitchen was placed under the mezzaine where the ceiling is lower. The mezzanine accommodates a new master bedroom, bathroom, and a home office. The new construction attempts to mediate between the unique character of the enclosing walls and the furniture, resembling a three-dimensional puzzle of interlocking views and spaces. Materials, colors, and details for the mezzanine were inspired by Stickley furniture to create a subtle transition between old and new.

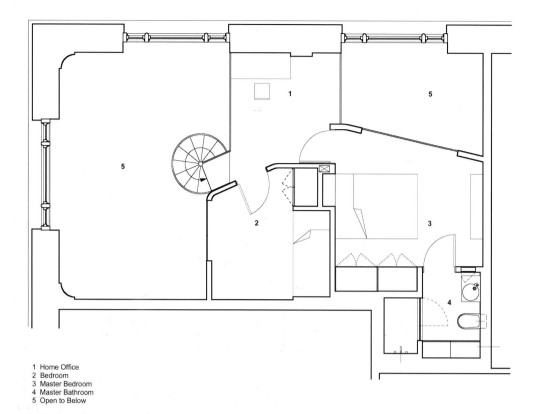

PREVIOUS PAGES: The
mezzanine opens to the
first floor.
RIGHT: The design for
the stair railing was
inspired by the client's
collection of Arts &
Crafts furniture.

1 Home Office
2 Bedroom
3 Master Bedroom
4 Master Bathroom
5 Open to Below

First-Floor Plan

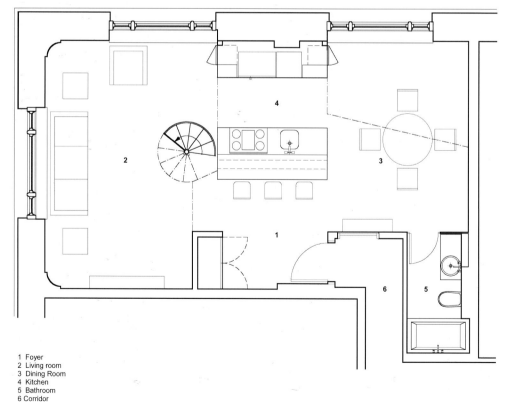

1 Foyer
2 Living room
3 Dining Room
4 Kitchen
5 Bathroom
6 Corridor

LEFT: The kitchen consists of a floating stainless steel island under the mezzanine.

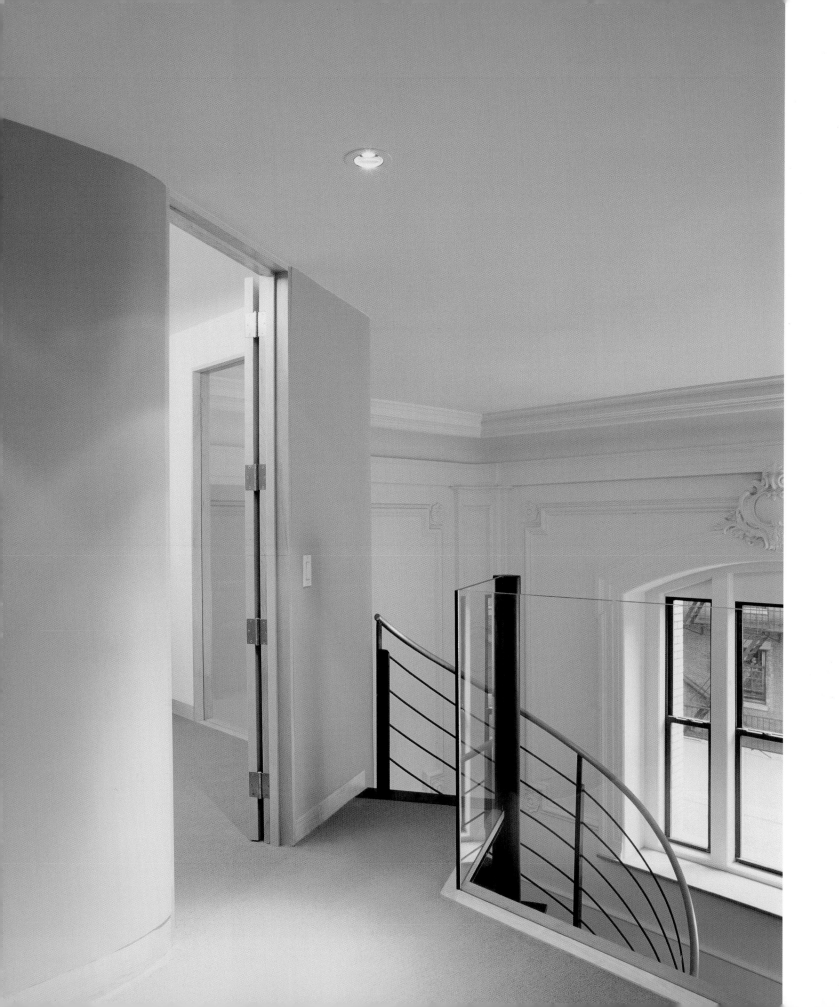

LEFT: A view from the mezzanine to the dining area. The original molding in the apartments was restored.

ABOVE AND LEFT: The material palette for the bathrooms consists of slate, onyx, and glass. Shown here is the first-floor bathroom.

EAGLE WAREHOUSE

ARCHITECT Michael Davis Architects **PHOTOGRAPHER** Ross Muir

THE EAGLE WAREHOUSE IS A TOP-FLOOR LOFT LOCATED in an 1874 Italianate storage building. The architect renovated the loft for himself. He exposed brick on the perimeter walls and discovered an additional four feet of space above a dropped drywall ceiling. The most striking feature in the apartment is the original 10-foot glass and iron clock face, which serves as the living room window— one of only two windows in the apartment. However, because of its top-floor location, the apartment is flooded with light from two barrel-vaulted skylights, one in the living room and the other in the bedroom.

Poised directly across from the eastern tower of the Brooklyn Bridge, the apartment commands an extraordinarily dramatic view of the East River and the skyline of lower Manhattan. In addition to acid-washed existing brick walls, the predominant materials are milk painted cabinets, tinted concrete counters, and variegated Asian slate. The apartment is furnished with English and American antiques and features a collection of rare Turkish and Central Asian carpets and textiles.

PREVIOUS PAGES: The unusually high ceilings allow the architect to extend the height of the book cases to accommodate an extensive library in a tight space.
RIGHT: Kitchen cabinets double as display cabinets.

FOLLOWING PAGES: When the architect purchased the apartment, the clock face was partially hidden by the dropped ceiling, and the metal brackets holding it in place were behind drywall. Now it is the focal point of the apartment and provides a panoramic view of the city, including a view of the Brooklyn Bridge.

Floor Plan

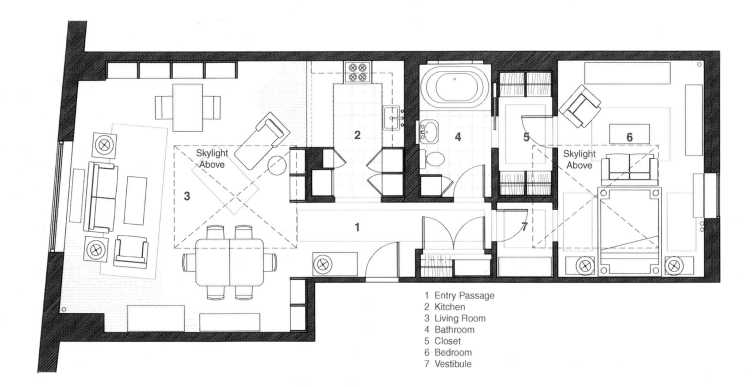

Skylight Above

Skylight Above

1 Entry Passage
2 Kitchen
3 Living Room
4 Bathroom
5 Closet
6 Bedroom
7 Vestibule

LEFT: The bathroom
is tiled in variegated
Asian slate.
ABOVE: While the
bedroom has only one
window, a vaulted skylight
brings in ample light.

DEEP FOCUS APARTMENT

ARCHITECT aardvarchitecture PHOTOGRAPHER Paúl Rivera/Archphoto, Billy Cunningham

THE SPATIAL QUALITY OF THIS PROJECT WAS determined by a series of views threaded through the existing rooms. The apartment, located on the top floor of a turn-of-the-century building, had the structure of a railroad flat. The architects' intervention was inspired by a an element in the building's plan, where the two ends of the apartment engage each other through small, facing windows. In order to open the small apartment spatially while leaving its inherent character intact, the architects created a series of cut-outs in the same north-south direction as these windows, beginning with a framed pass-through in the kitchen. The cut-outs continue through the shower, which is perforated by two windows, through the study, and into the master bedroom.

In an effort to balance the turn-of-the-century design with the new, modern construction, the architects decided to leave, but bleach the existing wainscotting. While the spatial structure and new woodwork are clearly modern and open, the wainscotting and the structure of the rooms are reminders of the apartment's original design. At the entry, a structural column clad in stainless steel and an entry cabinet with a fretted glass screen provide a balance of separation and continuity between entry, living room, and primary circulation.

Floor Plan

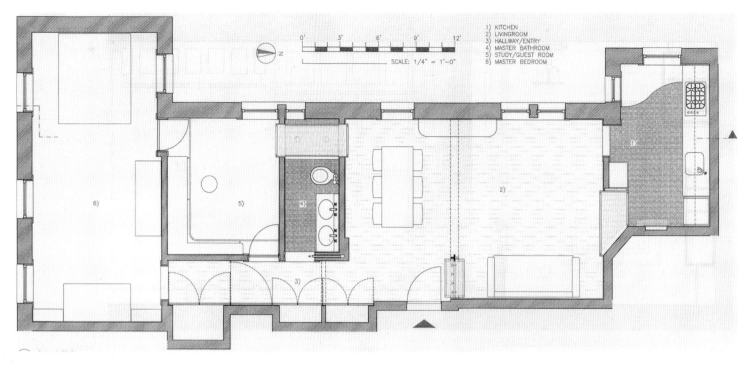

SCALE: 1/4" = 1'-0"

1) KITCHEN
2) LIVINGROOM
3) HALLWAY/ENTRY
4) MASTER BATHROOM
5) STUDY/GUEST ROOM
6) MASTER BEDROOM

Section

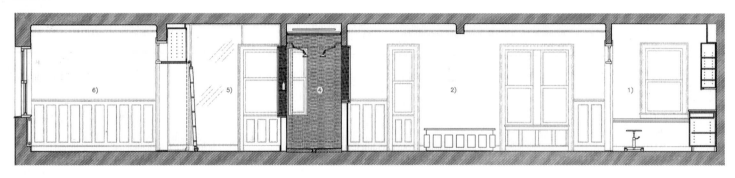

PREVIOUS PAGES: The living room offers a view of the kitchen and the pass-through to the right. Existing wainscoting and framing were bleached, giving the apartment a more contemporary feel. RIGHT: Detail of the kitchen pass-through

RIGHT: A stainless
steel-clad structural
column and a cabinet
with a fretted glass
screen mark the entry.

ABOVE: A view of the living room from the kitchen RIGHT: The design of this apartment was inspired by the cut-out windows that mark the apartment's boundaries.

LEFT AND ABOVE: In the study, adjacent to the bathroom, is a cut-out that provides a view through the shower to the living room. It consists of a privacy glass that can be electronically changed from clear to opaque with the flick of a switch.

ABOVE: The bathroom is clad with a light, neutral tile and a vivid gold-tinged blend in the shower.

FAR LEFT: A view of the bedroom with original wood mouldings

BOTTOM LEFT: A view through the privacy glass from the shower to the living room

WAXTER APARTMENT

ARCHITECT Slade Architects PHOTOGRAPHER Jordi Miralles

THE SECRET TO MAKING THIS "STRAIGHT" STUDIO apartment appear to be larger than its actual size is taking full advantage of the uncommonly generous number of windows that the apartment's corner location affords. Even the pullman kitchen is washed in natural light from a sliver of a window on the side.

The client, an art dealer, wanted an elegant space to showcase his art collection. A soft, monochromatic backdrop throughout the apartment allows the art to dominate. The kitchen counters are finished in white Corian and the glass cabinet doors reflect light from the side window. Simple, translucent window shades for light control adorn the windows. The architects established loose, flexible areas to accommodate sleeping, entertaining, and cooking.

Floor Plan

PREVIOUS PAGES:
Ample windows, a
monochromatic palette,
and simple, geometric
furniture visually expands
the space.
RIGHT BELOW: In the
kitchen, glass-fronted
cabinets reflect light from
a narrow side window.

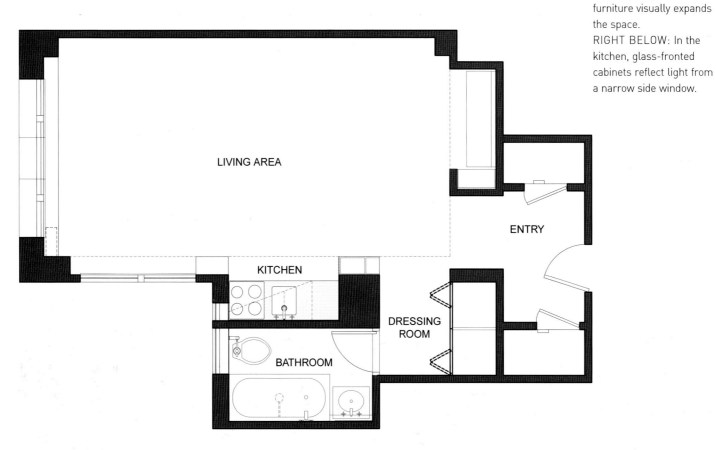

LIVING AREA

ENTRY

KITCHEN

DRESSING
ROOM

BATHROOM

Section

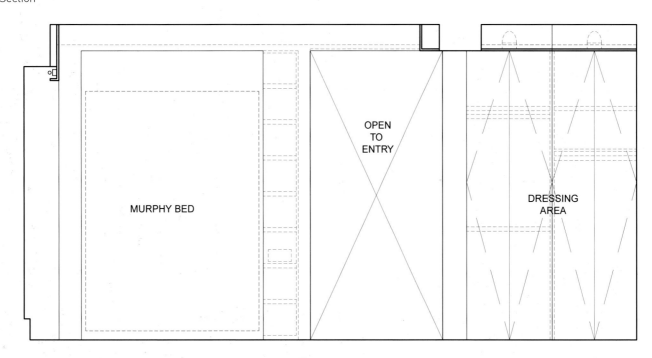

MURPHY BED

OPEN
TO
ENTRY

DRESSING
AREA

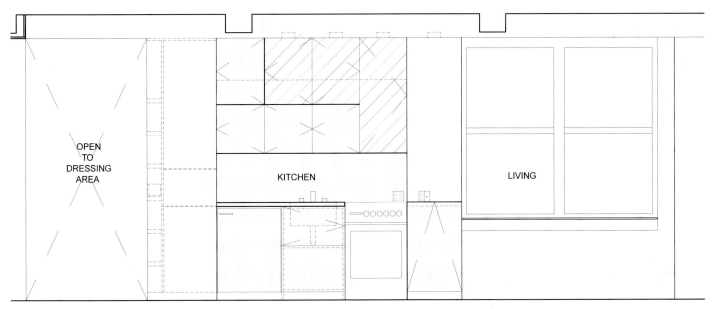

OPEN
TO
DRESSING
AREA

KITCHEN

LIVING

LEFT: Cove lighting along the length of the apartment adds to the sense of spaciousness. The wire side chairs and table appear to float in the space.

LEFT: The sleeping area as viewed from the living area
ABOVE: A view of the living area from the bed
RIGHT: When not in use, the bed folds into the wall, opening up space for entertaining.

LEFT: The entry as seen from the living and kitchen areas
RIGHT: Light is drawn into the kitchen from the narrow slide window.
BELOW RIGHT: The bathroom as seen from the dressing room; a mirror expands the space, reflecting the sleeping area beyond.

SEIDMON APARTMENT

ARCHITECT Stephen Alton **PHOTOGRAPHER** Eduard Hueber/Archphoto

THIS LOFT WAS CONFIGURED AND DETAILED TO ALLOW for privacy without losing the sense of a large open loft. The plan of the apartment was developed to allow the limited natural light of the living and kitchen areas at the front of the apartment to reach the bedroom and study at the rear of the space. This was accomplished by using sliding glass and steel doors with clear upper panes and translucent lower panes as space dividers. This configuration allows light to reach the rear of the space while providing privacy.

Wall and cabinetry units run the length of the apartment. These units are cantilevered work surfaces made of industrial lab top materials. The tops are attached to an industrial plastic resin coated plywood. Clerestory windows and the upper panels of the sliding screen effect a continuous ceiling plane.

A large volume clad in anagre wood paneling contains the kitchen, powder room, and laundry, organizing these "wet" functional requirements into one space.

Floor Plan

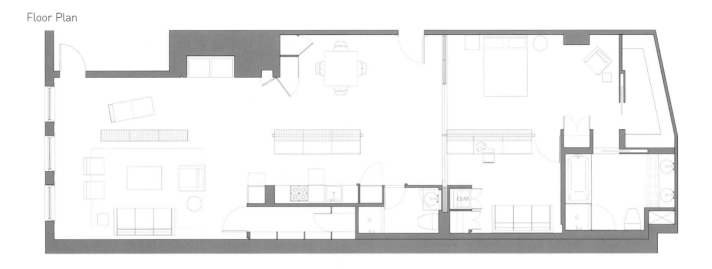

Axonometric

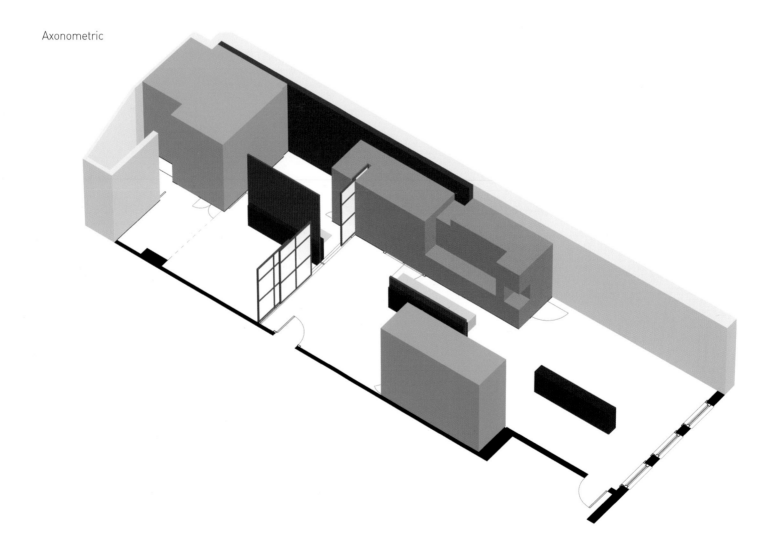

PREVIOUS PAGES: Natural light from the front of the loft reaches the windowless rear through clear and translucent sliding glass walls.

ABOVE: The wooden volume to the right contains the kitchen, powder room, and laundry room.

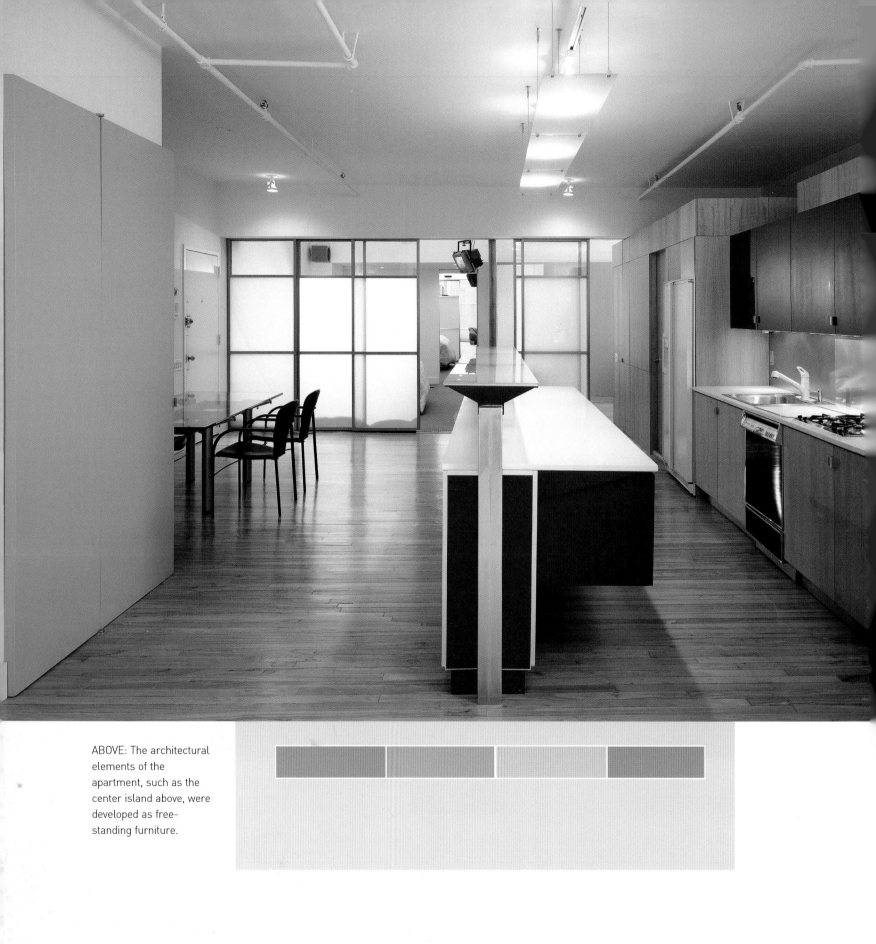

ABOVE: The architectural
elements of the
apartment, such as the
center island above, were
developed as free-
standing furniture.

LEFT AND ABOVE:
Anagre wood paneling
defines the kitchen area.
Cabinets do not reach the
ceiling, allowing it to read
as a continuous plane,

making the apartment
seem larger.
RIGHT: The luminescent
backsplash in the kitchen
adds depth to the counters.

RIGHT: Although windowless, the bedroom is bathed in natural light, transmitted through the translucent wall.

WHITE SPACE

ARCHITECT **Hanrahan + Meyers Architects** PHOTOGRAPHER **Michael Moran**

THE RENOVATION OF THIS APARTMENT FOCUSED ON opening the space and orienting it toward views of Central Park, which are primarily from the master bedroom and second bath. The existing space was gutted and reconfigured as a white box, based on a series of whites that are presented as variations in tone and texture. The variations are created by sandblasted, painted wood; wire brushed, painted wood; matte and polished plaster walls; floors whitened by bleaching and staining over oak plank; and floors finished with honed white marble tile. A translucent glass wall divides the living room from the new master bathroom. This wall brings light into the living room and visually connects it with the windows that overlook the park. Along the windowless and irregular south wall, the architects placed a series of wood panels that become closet doors. This provides needed storage while creating the illusion of straightening the wall.

Near the entrance, the wall becomes an area of low storage units with stainless steel shelves above. A free-form piece of ash sits on these low cabinets, forming a counter. A raised floor area at the entrance includes the kitchen, separated from the dining area and entrance space by a freestanding translucent glass wall. The dining area was created by continuing the kitchen counter through the glass wall where it becomes the dining room table. The existing raised floor was too small to allow seating on both sides of the table so the architects extended it with a clear structural glass floor. It floats above a free-form ash step, connecting the entrance to the living area.

Floor Plan

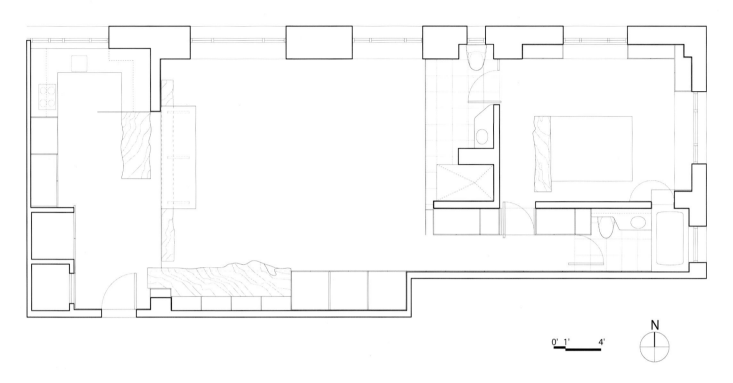

N

0' 1'   4'

PREVIOUS PAGES: The
bedroom is lined with
painted wood panels on
the south and west walls,
and plaster surfaces on
the north and east walls.
The architects designed
the furniture in the
bedroom, which are made
of wire brushed solid
wood with a high gloss
white lacquer finish. A
free-form piece of ash sits
on top of the bed
headboard.
LEFT: A detail of the
bedroom wall
RIGHT AND FAR RIGHT:
A free-form piece of ash
functions as a step into
the living room and as a
bookshelf. Structural
glass extends the raised
dining-area floor.

PREVIOUS PAGES: A view of the translucent glass wall separating the master bath from the living area, as seen from the raised glass floor of the dining area

ABOVE AND RIGHT: The dining table is an extension of the kitchen counter through the translucent glass wall dividing the spaces.

ABOVE: The entry to the
master bathroom with the
translucent glass wall
beyond right
RIGHT: The shower is
separated from the
living area by the
translucent wall.

FAR RIGHT: Adjacent to
the master bedroom is a
soaking tub with
picture-perfect views of
Central Park.

FLAT IRON LOFT

ARCHITECT **Slade Architects** PHOTOGRAPHER **Jordi Miralles**

THOUGH LARGER THAN MOST APARTMENTS IN THIS book, ideas incorporated in the layout and materials selection for this project can be applied to the smallest apartments. This space has a rectangular floor plan, with windows on each of the short sides. Bringing light into the interior spaces was an important design goal and is a challenge faced by many apartment dwellers.

The entry vestibule sets the tone for the apartment with mid-century-style industrial glazing and a blackened steel frame. Translucent glass allows light into the vestibule. The slate floor has a small patch of live grass that takes advantage of the natural light. Upon entering the apartment, one faces the kitchen enclosure made of the same paneled glazing system as the foyer. The kitchen enclosure shields the kitchen from the entry but is open to the living/dining area.

An open corridor links the public area to the private bedroom/bathroom area. A series of spaces provide areas for the guest bathroom and home office, and line this corridor which terminates in the master bedroom suite. These spaces are separated by sliding or pivoting panels in a variety of translucent materials that include fiberglass, woven leather, and translucent glass.

Floor Plan

DINING   KITCHEN   PANTRY   GUEST BATH   BEDROOM   CLOSET

LIVING   ENTRY   MASTER BATH   MASTER BEDROOM

Sections

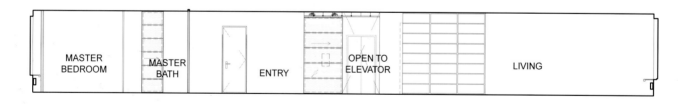

MASTER BEDROOM   MASTER BATH   ENTRY   OPEN TO ELEVATOR   LIVING

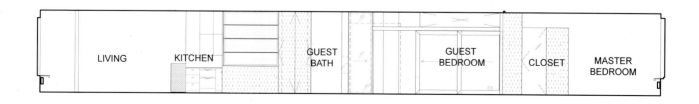

LIVING   KITCHEN   GUEST BATH   GUEST BEDROOM   CLOSET   MASTER BEDROOM

LEFT: A view of the living area with the sliding storage door in the closed position that allows light to enter the foyer through the translucent paneling
ABOVE: The storage unit/bar separating the dining area from the kitchen is mounted on rollers, allowing it to be shifted easily to open the kitchen fully, extending the living space and allowing different configurations whenever entertaining demands.

ABOVE: The face of the storage unit/bar is a translucent acrylic panel that looks opaque from the living/dining areas and allows natural light into the cabinet on the kitchen side.

LEFT AND RIGHT: The kitchen cabinetry is made of multi-ply maple plywood with black Richlite counters. This material is a composite product of recycled paper.

LEFT: The guest room is separated from the corridor by a wooden frame with an infill woven in leather. The master bedroom is at the end of the corridor.
ABOVE: The guest bathroom

LEFT: A translucent glass panel separates the master bedroom from the master bath, allowing light into the bath area. RIGHT: In the bathroom the sink is solid onyx, lit from below. It spans across the width of the space in front of the glass wall. Opposite the bath is a walk-in closet paneled in maple that ends two feet short of the ceiling, to allow natural light into the dressing area and allow for a more open feeling to the room.

DUPLEX APARTMENT

ARCHITECT Chelsea Atelier PHOTOGRAPHER Björg Magnea

IDENTICAL APARTMENTS STACKED ON THE THIRD AND fourth floor of this building were combined into a single duplex unit. The existing apartment units were small, very narrow, and had low ceiling height. The design challenge was to transform this narrow space into an open and spacious apartment. Part of the upper floor was carved out to connect it to the lower level via new metal stairs made of steel sheets bent into continuous folds and cantilevered from the wall, making them appear almost weightless. The ceiling above the dining area was also removed, creating a strong visual connection between the first and second floors.

While working within a tight envelope, the architects were able to accommodate a remarkably rich program through the use of glass walls and multifunctional open spaces. The upper floor contains the master bedroom, a children's room that overlooks the dining area through a glass partition, and a private audio-visual room surrounded by glass walls. On the lower floor, the kitchen overlooks the dining and living areas. The existing bedroom was divided, forming a guest bedroom and a study. It was surrounded with low partitions topped with glass to permit daylight into the room.

Second-Floor Plan

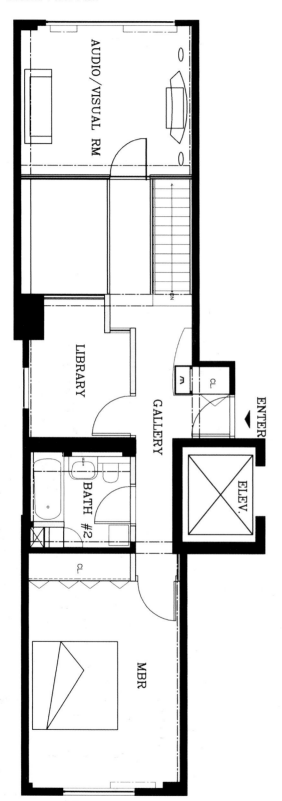

AUDIO/VISUAL RM.

LIBRARY

GALLERY

BATH #2

CL.

ENTER

ELEV.

CL.

MBR

First-Floor Plan

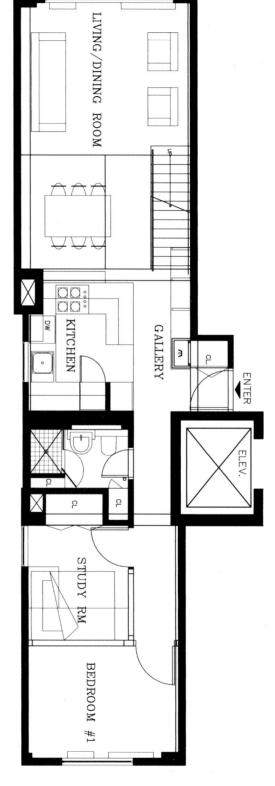

LIVING/DINING ROOM

UP

DW

KITCHEN

GALLERY

CL.

ENTER

CL.

CL.

ELEV.

STUDY RM.

BEDROOM #1

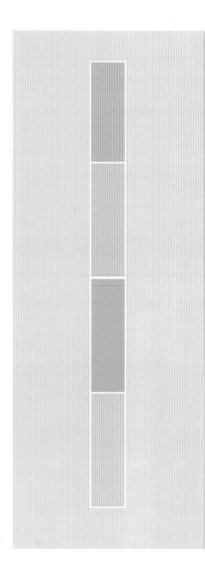

PREVIOUS PAGES: A staircase made of bent sheet steel connects the combined apartments. RIGHT: The ceiling above the dining room was removed to create a visual connection with the upstairs.

LEFT AND ABOVE: The
living room as seen from
the kitchen area and from
the upstairs landing

ABOVE: The master bedroom
LEFT: To maintain a feeling
of openness, glass railings
and walls are used on the
upstairs island that connects
the master bedroom with the
stairs and media room.

NOHO LOFT

ARCHITECT Slade Architects PHOTOGRAPHER Jordi Miralles

THIS LIVE/WORK LOFT APARTMENT WAS DESIGNED FOR an active, young couple who are professional photographers. The existing apartment had beautiful, high ceilings but limited light, since all the windows were located along one wall. The new design takes full advantage of these windows by placing partial height or translucent walls perpendicular to them in order to bring light deep into the apartment.

The kitchen work areas were arranged in a bar along the perimeter, which allowed the floor space to remain open for entertaining. The home office and workspace is tucked behind the entry vestibule with a guest sleeping area above. The built-in desk features a light table with a steel wall behind it. This wall provides a visual accent and also a place to put up photos and memos with magnets. The main wall dividing the public space from the private bedroom area is made from translucent fiberglass panels on a wood frame. This material allows natural light into the master bedroom. The materials in the bedroom are lighter and the palette is warmer. The bathroom includes a large Jacuzzi bath and shower. A custom-made poured-resin sink stretches the length of the vanity and becomes a glass enclosure into the bedroom.

PREVIOUS PAGES: The center of the loft was kept open for entertaining. The master bedroom is located behind the translucent bookcase wall. The entry to the apartment is to the right.

Floor Plan

LAUNDRY/
STORAGE

ENTRY

OFFICE

GUEST
BATH

MASTER
BATH

KITCHEN/
DINING

LIBRARY

BEDROOM

LIVING
AREA

Kitchen Section

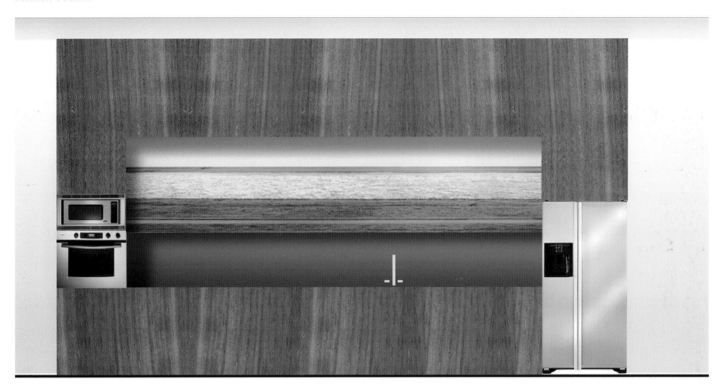

Translucent Wall Section

ABOVE AND LEFT: The kitchen was placed against the wall to maximize the open space at the entry.

RIGHT: The entry as seen from the kitchen

FOLLOWING PAGES: The apartment's only windows are along the living area wall. By making the back of the bookcase translucent, light is able to enter the bedroom behind.

LEFT: Internal
fluorescent lighting
illuminates the bookcase.
ABOVE: Flat metal filing
cases provide storage
for photographs.
FOLLOWING PAGES: A
view of the kitchen from
the living area

LEFT: A view of the master
bedroom encased behind
the translucent wall
ABOVE: Entry to the
master bathroom

LEFT, BELOW, AND
RIGHT: The bathroom
includes a large Jacuzzi
bath and shower. The
lowered ceiling area in
the bathroom is
accentuated and offset by
a vaulted void over the
tub and toilet. A solid
custom-made, poured-
resin sink stretches the
length of the vanity and
becomes a glass
enclosure into the
bedroom, with natural
light on one side and the
shower on the other.

VAN DOREN RESIDENCE

ARCHITECT Cho Slade Architects PHOTOGRAPHER Jordi Miralles

THIS TWO STORY APARTMENT WAS DESIGNED TO BE A pied-a-terre for an art dealer. The apartment is organized into an open living and entertainment space on the first floor with a combined bedroom and home office above. In the entry, a sculpted, curved plaster wall unifies the space and emphasizes the window opening in the entry. The first floor powder room and kitchen are contained within a seamless box covered with Sapele wood paneling. Inside the box, the kitchen is clad entirely in pale green Corian. In the powder room, the sink, countertop, and ceiling are made of solid white Corian. The walls are a translucent white glass that is backlit to provide a light for the space.

Upstairs, a built-in desk unit provides ample space for two people to work and divides the open space into two zones: the main bedroom area and a small corner alcove with a built-in, upholstered seating area for reading and watching TV. Translucent glass at all the openings on this level allows light to penetrate the master bedroom and closet as well as the stairwell.

Second-Floor Plan

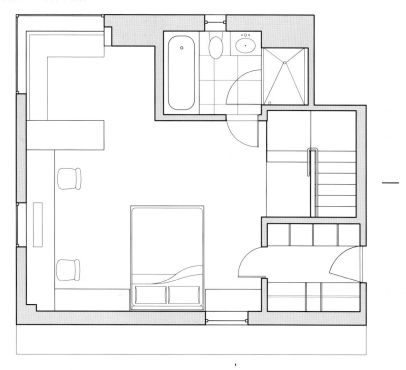

PREVIOUS PAGES: The
kitchen and powder
room are enclosed
within a box paneled with
Sapele. The floors and
stair treads are teak.
BELOW RIGHT: The stair
treads are cantilevered
from the wall, reducing
the mass of the staircase.

First-Floor Plan

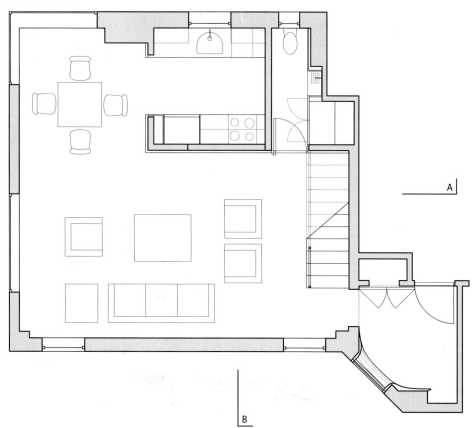

A

B

Sections

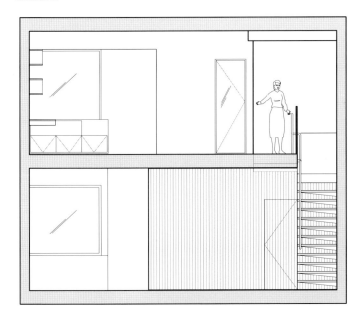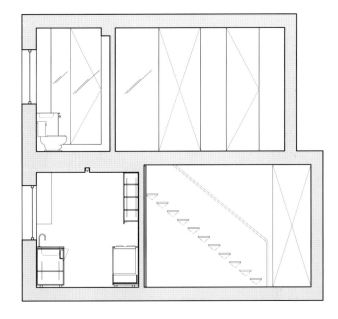

LEFT: The dining area
ABOVE: The kitchen's
interior is clad in pale
green Corian.

LEFT: The apartment
is elegantly but simply
furnished.
ABOVE: A view of the
bedroom and office area
from the teak stairs

ABOVE AND RIGHT: A
built-in desk unit divides
the sleeping area from
an alcove for reading and
watching TV.

LEFT AND ABOVE: The powder room has back-lit translucent glass.
RIGHT: The apartment benefits from exposures on three sides.

McGRATH APARTMENT

ARCHITECT Anima **PHOTOGRAPHER** Paúl Rivera/Archphoto

THIS CHELSEA APARTMENT WAS CONVERTED FROM A typical railroad layout into a flexible work and living space. All existing room partitions were removed to create an uninterrupted open area as well as to allow natural light to flow into the center of this long, narrow space. The center of the apartment contains the living, dining, and kitchen areas while the master bedroom and the office/guest room are at the back and front of the apartment respectively.

Integrated sliding doors and furniture enhance the linearity and verticality of the space. The built-in closets disappear behind translucent glass doors and pocket doors. A fold-down bed converts the home office into a guest room. The custom-built, stainless steel kitchen with concealed appliances can be fully enclosed when required. An extremely small existing bathroom was remodeled into a condensed box of blue stone, mosaic, and translucent glass, efficient and atmospheric at the same time.

First-Floor Plan

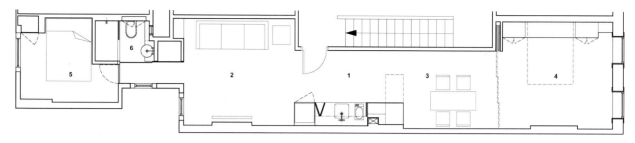

1 Foyer/ Pantry
2 Living Area
3 Dining Area
4 Home Office/ Bedroom
5 Master Bedroom
6 Bathroom

PREVIOUS PAGES AND LEFT: The stainless steel kitchen can be closed or open as shown left. RIGHT: The kitchen offers a view toward the dining area and home office/guest room. The monochromatic color scheme unifies the long, narrow space.

LEFT: A view toward the living area and master bedroom from the kitchen
FOLLOWING PAGES: The compact bathroom is a symphony of blue stone, mosaic, and translucent glass.

SIMPLIFIED CLASSIC

ARCHITECT Architecture In Formation PHOTOGRAPHER Matthew Bremer

THE RENOVATION OF THIS APARTMENT WAS GUIDED by the desire to edit, simplify, and reinterpret the 1000-square-foot space. Located in an early 1900s building designed by the noted architectural firm Bing and Bing, the apartment's classic lines and proportions were maintained while a new, rich palette of contemporary colors and textures where inserted. Walls separating the living room, dining room, foyer, and kitchen were eliminated to create an inviting and informal open space.

Storage and the separation of public and private spaces were major concerns in the remodeling of the apartment. Most of the apartment's walls were "thickened" to accommodate closets and cabinets in the living area and the bedroom, where an entertainment niche was inserted between two built-in closets. A dropped soffit in the bedroom was fashioned into a bookcase. Free-standing stainless steel cabinets define the kitchen and a stainless steel island separates it from the living area. A prized window over the integrated stainless steel sink frames a dramatic view of the Manhattan skyline.

Floor Plan

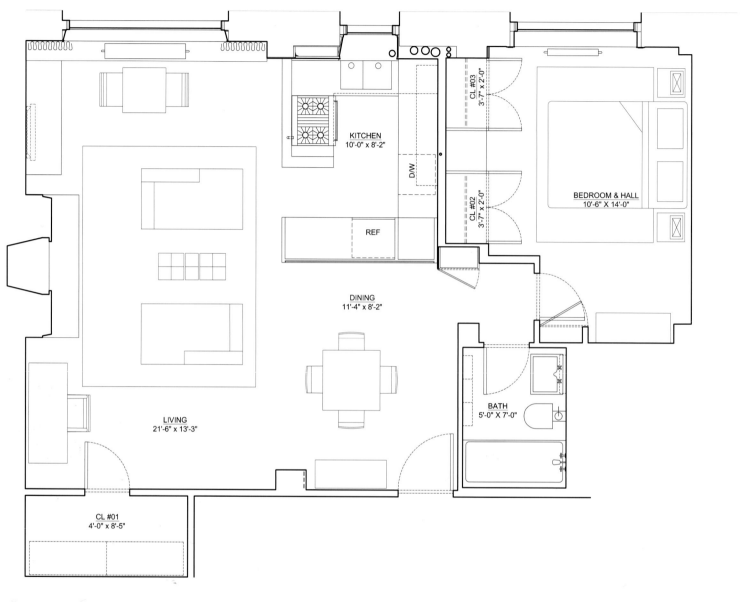

KITCHEN
10'-0" x 8'-2"

CL #03
3'-7" x 2'-0"

CL #02
3'-7" x 2'-0"

BEDROOM & HALL
10'-6" X 14'-0"

D/W

REF

DINING
11'-4" x 8'-2"

BATH
5'-0" X 7'-0"

LIVING
21'-6" x 13'-3"

CL #01
4'-0" x 8'-5"

PREVIOUS PAGES: A view of the living room from the foyer with the kitchen reflected in the mirror above the fireplace.
RIGHT: The walls separating the entry from the living area were removed. The stainless steel cabinets of the kitchen are to the left.

ABOVE AND RIGHT: The extremely intimate scale of the apartment required thoughtful integration of the architecture and furnishings.

ABOVE: A view of the dining room and built-ins along the window

RIGHT: A view from the entry looking into the bedroom suite

LEFT: The kitchen as
seen from the
living/dining area
ABOVE: The kitchen
window above the sink
looks out over the city.

LEFT: A handmade paper-maché wall adds a sense of depth and mystery to the bedroom.

ABOVE: A dropped soffit provides storage for books.